Santorini
Travel Guide

Quick Trips Series

No part of this publication may be reproduced, stored in a retrieval system, or transmitted, in any form or by any means without the prior written permission of the publisher, nor be otherwise circulated in any form of binding or cover other than that in which it is published and without similar condition being imposed on the subsequent purchaser. If there are any errors or omissions in copyright acknowledgements the publisher will be pleased to insert the appropriate acknowledgement in any subsequent printing of this publication. Although we have taken all reasonable care in researching this book we make no warranty about the accuracy or completeness of its content and disclaim all liability arising from its use.

Copyright © 2016, Astute Press
All Rights Reserved.

Table of Contents

SANTORINI 6
- 🌍 Customs & Culture 7
- 🌍 Geography 9
- 🌍 Weather & Best Time to Visit 11

SIGHTS & ACTIVITIES: WHAT TO SEE & DO 14
- 🌍 Oia 14
- 🌍 Amoudi Bay 15
- 🌍 Firá 16
- 🌍 Black Pebble Beach of Kamari 18
- 🌍 Winery Visits 19
- 🌍 Red Beach & White Beach, Akrotiri 21
- 🌍 Trail Hike from Fira to Oia 22
- 🌍 Museum of Prehistoric Thera, Firá 24
- 🌍 Akrotiri Ruins 25
- 🌍 Thirasia 27
- 🌍 Open Air Cinema, Kimari 28
- 🌍 Ancient Thera 29
- 🌍 Santorini Volcano 30
- 🌍 Thira Maritime Museum 31
- 🌍 Monastery of Profitis Ilias, Pyrgos 32

BUDGET TIPS 35

- **ACCOMMODATION** **35**
  - Zorzis Hotel, Perissa 35
  - Mediterranean Beach Hotel, Kamari 36
  - Katikies, Oia 37
  - Caldera's Lillum Villa, Fira 37
  - 160° Thea Hotel, Oia 38
- **RESTAURANTS, CAFÉS & BARS** **39**
  - Palla Kameni Cocktail Bar, Fira 40
  - 1800 Restaurant, Oia 40
  - Roka, Oia 41
  - Dimitris, Ammoudi 42
  - Archipelagos, Fira 43
- **SHOPPING** **43**
  - Kostas Antoniou, Fira 44
  - Iama, Oia 45
  - Galateas Pottery Studio, Megalochori 46
  - Atlantis Bookstore, Oia 47
  - Beach Promenade, Kamari 47

KNOW BEFORE YOU GO 49

- **ENTRY REQUIREMENTS** **49**
- **HEALTH INSURANCE** **49**
- **TRAVELLING WITH PETS** **50**
- **AIRPORTS** **50**
- **AIRLINES** **52**
- **CURRENCY** **53**
- **BANKING & ATMS** **53**
- **CREDIT CARDS** **53**
- **TOURIST TAXES** **54**
- **RECLAIMING VAT** **54**

- **Tipping Policy** 55
- **Mobile Phones** 55
- **Dialling Code** 56
- **Emergency Numbers** 56
- **Public Holidays** 57
- **Time Zone** 57
- **Daylight Savings Time** 58
- **School Holidays** 58
- **Trading Hours** 58
- **Driving Laws** 59
- **Drinking Laws** 60
- **Smoking Laws** 60
- **Electricity** 60
- **Tourist Information (TI)** 61
- **Food & Drink** 62
- **Websites** 63

SANTORINI TRAVEL GUIDE

Santorini

From the ashes of a great volcanic eruption arose the exotic Greek island of Santorini. The romantic island, named for Saint Irene, is located in the glistening Aegean Sea and is famous for its spectacular views, gorgeous beaches, impressive mountains and vibrant sunsets.

SANTORINI TRAVEL GUIDE

The island has an enormous basin of water, the only sunken caldera in the world. The large developments on the island, Firá, and Oia, have been constructed to complement this natural wonder. The city of Oia dazzles the viewer in the sunlight with its charming blue-domed churches, and the capital city, Firá, with its white-walled domiciles and ancient structures.

Visitors to Santorini can relax in the Aegean sun, sip local varieties of wine at one of many of the exceptional wineries, hike in the glorious mountains, or tour ancient ruins in the volcanic ash. Santorini is a paradise beyond expectations, offering entertainment options for every taste and personality. If you're looking for breathtaking views of the Aegean Sea, Santorini is one of the best places to be. If you enjoy exciting nightlife scenes, it's got that too. Beaches, volcanos, and endless horizon can be found on Santorini.

🌐 Customs & Culture

The culture of Santorini has evolved tremendously over the last few centuries, from a subsistent agrarian society, to Greek Orthodox community, to bustling modern city complete with eclectic nightclubs and entertainment scenes. But, ultimately, Santorini is a culture of contrasts, of styles both old and new. It boasts ancient architecture, hearkening back to the Ottoman and Minoan Empires, and contemporary shopping and restaurants.

It's no wonder that archaeologists have considered Santorini to be the lost city of Atlantis, the landscape is harshly beautiful, from spectacular volcanos to dazzling beaches. The people who have survived here, the natives who call this place their own, are a strong people. Not even ten years ago, Santorini was struggling economically, their island continually wrecked by

SANTORINI TRAVEL GUIDE

earthquakes and volcanic eruptions. But they weren't put off, they built and re-built their lives from the ashes. And they accomplished this to such success that Santorini was picked as the world's best island by Travel + Leisure magazine in 2011.

Also, thanks to its semi-arid climate and proximity to the Sea, Santorini boasts an extensive wine culture. Vineyards speckle the horizon from Kamari to Thira, each with their own distinctive specialties. The local passion for wine is just one more decadent element to the sweetness of the island, presenting a lifestyle of indulgence and incredible taste.

Santorini exists as a world apart from the mainland of Greece. When the rest of Greece was struggling economically, Santorini was thriving. Even in the worst of

SANTORINI TRAVEL GUIDE

times people love Santorini, because it offers a refuge, an escape not easily found throughout the rest of the region. The island offers a carefree life, with quaint outdoor cafés with locals and visitors alike sharing a meal in the sun, and beaches inviting individuals to bask in the glow of the Aegean.

🌍 Geography

Santorini is revered just as much for its unusual geography and geology as it is for its exceptional beauty. The island of Santorini is southernmost part of the Cycladic group of islands in the Aegean Sea, and is a crescent shaped archipelago. Santorini refers in name to more than just the one island, but also to the municipality that includes the nearby islands of Therasia among others. It is approximately 200 km southeast of the Grecian mainland.

SANTORINI TRAVEL GUIDE

The peculiar geology was formed by the Minoan (Thera) Eruption of almost 3600 years ago (circa the 17th century B.C.). The bodies of land were shaped by the collapse of the volcanic caldera, pushing the layers of volcanic ash higher and higher. The diversity of sand on the beaches at Santorini reflects this layering, and the variant colors are as a result of the different levels of present ash exposure. The magnificence of Santorini is shaped by the volcanic caldera surrounding the masses of land, the world's only sunken caldera at a depth of 400m. Between the islands is a shimmering lagoon, surrounded on three sides by the hovering cliffs of the Santorini mainlands.

Like other Cycladic Islands, the architecture of Santorini was developed from the native stone and whitewashed to withstand the elements. Situated on the cliffside is the

SANTORINI TRAVEL GUIDE

capital city of Firá (Also spelled Thira or Thera), its aubergine walls shining in the Grecian light. The native population is recorded at about 13,500 people, but the actual number of people there differs greatly throughout the course of the year, as it is an extremely busy port in late spring and summer.

🌍 Weather & Best Time to Visit

Santorini, along with nearby Anafi, are the only two locations in Europe that possess a truly hot desert climate, but this is only just. The island has a Mediterranean climate but with slightly warmer temperatures throughout the year. Like most of the Mediterranean region, Santorini has two main seasons, a wet season and a dry season. Thus, in the spring and summer the climate is predominately warm to hot and sees little to no rain, and in the fall and winter

SANTORINI TRAVEL GUIDE

temperatures are mild and there is generally more precipitation. Average temperatures in the dry season range from 17 to 27 degrees Celsius, and in the wet from 12-21 degrees Celsius. So, although it never gets too cold here, light jackets are sometimes needed.

The sun shines brightly throughout the year in Santorini, warming the Aegean Sea. The water stays at a temperature of around 70 degrees from June to October, allowing for idyllic swimming conditions for most of the year. June-August is the height of the tourist season, and thousands of cruise ships stop at Fira for port-of-call. It's possible to go a bit earlier, but the evenings do remain about chilly in May and March.

The absolute best time to be in Santorini, however, is in September and October. The tourists have gone home,

SANTORINI TRAVEL GUIDE

rain is hardly seen, and the waters of the Aegean are still warm and inviting. And, although prices are high in Santorini throughout the year, at this time, because demand is less, things are slightly cheaper.

SANTORINI TRAVEL GUIDE

Sights & Activities: What to See & Do

 Oia

Postcard perfect Oia (pronounced "Ia") stands luxuriously on the cliffs of Santorini, and is the most famous village on the island. The winding, picturesque streets complete with quaint bistros and cafés, invite the visitor to linger for a while, drinking in the horizon. During the summer the tiny spot becomes a sort of metropolis, with day-trippers going here and there, the region transforms into a center of incredible activity. But in the fall, and lasting through winter, Oia opens up to those who wish to know it. It becomes serene again, tranquil as it was intended to be.

The most famous sights in Oia are the blue-domed churches, a delightful contrast to the pristine pearl walls of the city. But no matter what season you visit Oia, it continues to offer the charm of the old world and the comfort of the new. It is a haven for artists, writers, musicians, and travelers alike; individuals seeking for a solitary space of ineffable beauty.

Many of the island's cultural attractions call Oia their home, in addition to a number of shops, excellent seafood restaurants, and spectacular views of the Aegean. The character, the mindset, the perspective of Santorini is realized here, and thus, a trip to the island is incomplete without a stop in Oia.

🌐 Amoudi Bay

Oia's own Amoudi Bay is usually the first place recommended by past visitors when asked about the best of Santorini, ultimately it is often perceived as the most beautiful place on the island. In the northeastern sector,

SANTORINI TRAVEL GUIDE

Amoudi Bay is a sparkling cove complete with tiny beach, and otherwise a perfect place to view the famous Mediterranean sunset. The area used to be the island's main commercial port, but is now an enclave of Santorini culture and style. Getting to the area is a bit of an adventure all to itself, and although you can take a scooter or car, more exciting options include riding a donkey the way the natives used to, or descending the steep 300 steps from the hovering magical town of Oia overhead.

No matter how you get there, once you've arrived you're instantly immersed in the sights of the Aegean, and sounds of quiet activity. The Bay entrance is lined with dozens of tavernas and small, unique shops, perfect for a lazy afternoon of wandering and exploring. Although challenging, it's even possible to swim here, giving brave souls the opportunity to enjoy the water in the stunning Caldera. But whether you wish to be in the sea, view the radiant sunset, or grab a drink along the coast, Amoudi Bay is someplace you'll want to be while in Santorini.

🌐 Firá

The capital city of Firá is the center of the excitement in Santorini. This historic town hosts the widest variety of shops, restaurants, and entertainment options that can be found on the island of Santorini. It is located on the western edge of the island, and offers extraordinary views of the caldera and the tiny volcanic island of Nea Kameni. This is usually the first place visitors see on the island, and is connected to the water by a series of cable cars. The architecture stylings of Firá are similar to that of Oia, with aubergine walls and azure rooftops; but Firá sports a scene much more dynamic then that of its neighbor.

SANTORINI TRAVEL GUIDE

During the day, visitors can join natives meeting over a glass of wine at tavernas in Theotokopoulou Square, stroll the city streets, and shop at many of the boutiques and jewelry stores along the main drag. Because it is situated 260m above the blue caldera, Firá's many restaurants and accommodations sport amazing views of the sunken volcano. And thus, in spite of the common bustle, visitors can escape for a while from the noise of the city to a quiet space enveloped by beauty.

At night, the nightclubs open, transforming the center of the city into a large party. This is especially the case in Spring and Summer as students make their way to the Grecian coast for a good time. But, if this isn't your scene, there are plenty of quiet places available so that you can enjoy your vacation in serenity. In Firá, wandering days turn into exciting nights, and whether you're a history buff or the life of the party, Firá is a unique destination that offers a little bit of everything.

🌍 Black Pebble Beach of Kamari

The island of Santorini is full of natural wonders formed as a result of the Minoan volcanic eruption of 3600 B.C. One of these incredible formations can be found in Kamari at the unusual black pebble beach. The "sand" is formed by granulated course volcanic sand that's so peculiar that you'll have to see it to believe it. The black sand adjacent to the cool blue water is a magnificent sight to behold. Come lay in the sun, or swim in the salubrious waters, and experience it for yourself.

The Black Pebble Beach of Kamari is a certified Blue Flag beach, an award granted by the Foundation for

SANTORINI TRAVEL GUIDE

Environmental Education for cleanliness and quality. The beach is also equipped with fantastic amenities for guests, including umbrellas and sun beds for hire, numerous fruit stands, and exciting water sports opportunities (water skiing, diving, etc.).

Kamari is an exceptionally relaxed environment, as many daytrippers don't have the opportunity to make it out this far while on vacation in Santorini. And after a day on the beach, and you feel you've had enough of the sun, there's a promenade alongside the Pebble Beach with tavernas, shops, and cafés for your convenience and enjoyment.

🌐 Winery Visits

P.O. Box 23020, Oia TK 84702, Greece

+ 30 22860 71474

http://www.santorinifoodwine.com/

SANTORINI TRAVEL GUIDE

One of the highlights of any trip to Santorini is an excursion into its unique gastronomy. The island grows, in addition to its very popular cherry tomatoes, a series of indigenous grapes. And from these exceptional fruits comes one of the island's leading industries, wine.

In the late 1980s something extraordinary happened on the island of Santorini, people began to realize its vast agrarian potential. Vineyards that had been long abandoned, were reopened, cultivated, and brought forth in all of their glory. The primary grape that grows on Santorini is the Assyrtikos variety, a succulent, versatile fruit that translates well into white wine. Santorini typical white wines are dry and acerbic, with mineral and citrus hues that speak to the features of the volcanic island itself. Dessert wines are known as "visanto," which is traditionally sweet and commonly seen in Santorini.

The volcanic soil itself is mineral rich, giving life to the vines of Santorini. A tour of a local vineyard is a decadent exploration of this unique offering, and an up-close opportunity of visiting the authentic side of the island. Whether you are an oenophile, a connoisseur, or simply someone who likes wine with dinner, visiting a winery in Santorini is an enriching, refreshing experience that's as memorable as it is delicious.

🌎 Red Beach & White Beach, Akrotiri

There's more to see at Akrotiri than the ancient ruins, the small development hosts some of the most unique beaches on the entire island. Where hues of vibrant

SANTORINI TRAVEL GUIDE

crimson, scarlet, amber combine on the impressive red beach; the absence of color on the white beach accomplishes the same.

Red Beach, Kokkini Paralia, is not the sort of place to lounge in the water or on the sand catching some rays, Santorini is full of places such as these. Instead, it is a stunning view not often seen anywhere else on earth, with bright water and red pumice stones. Situated adjacent to the quiet town of Akrotiri, Kokkini is a photographer's haven. Although it takes some effort to get to, the hiking of a rocky trail to be precise, it's more than worth it for what's there. And plus, this area is the home for some of the most affordable tavernas on the island.

It's magnificent counterpart, white beach, is accessible via boat from Kokkin Paralia for approximately €5 round trip.

It is undoubtedly the most secluded beach in Santorini, with plenty of places to relax with breathtaking views of the horizon. The water is clean, the beach is wide, and the surrounding cliffs add the perfect exotic touch.

For idyllic settings in a secluded space, Akrotiri's beaches are unmatched.

🌏 Trail Hike from Fira to Oia

This ethereal cliffside hike from Fira to Oia is not to be reversed, as it is only in this direction that the views are truly transcendent. The overall journey takes approximately 3.5 hours, with plenty of opportunities to stop along the way. The trail goes through the town of Imerovigli, the renowned 'balcony of the Aegean." Historically, because of its great height, this village was

SANTORINI TRAVEL GUIDE

the spot from which natives would watch pirate ships entering the caldera.

This hike is certainly not for the fainthearted, however, at some points the trail becomes steep and rocky, and at many places there is no rail between the path and the cliffside. But, the existence of this trail proves that the island of Santorini is not solely dedicated to luxury, the island offers entertainment for those with a sense of adventure as well. And, ultimately, this trek is more than worth the effort.

As you begin the trail, the first landmark you'll come across is the Cycladic church of Profitis, from there you commence the trail in the shade of the mountainous overhang to the right, and full view of the sea to the left. For the next two miles the trail will rotate between smooth flat and rocky cliffside, with numerous opportunities to stop and take pictures along the way. Then at last, you'll near the old city of Oia, where the trail will be covered with white mountain ash, a magical wonderland of Santorini.

🌐 Museum of Prehistoric Thera, Firá

Mitropoleos St., Fira 847 00, Greece

30 22860 23217

http://www.santorini.gr-santorini.com/museums/prehistoric_museum.htm

Many people don't come to Santorini for the museums, and as a result they miss out on one of the island's premiere cultural experiences, the Museum of Prehistoric Thera. You can find it in the capital city of Firá, and the

SANTORINI TRAVEL GUIDE

exhibitions boast indigenous findings from the Cycladic and Neolithic Periods. It is separated into four segments: History of Thera Research, Geology, History from the Late Neolithic to the Late Cycladic Periods, and the lost city of Akrotiri.

The ancient island of Thera was a Minoan epicenter during the Bronze Age, and many artifacts from this rich era are housed in the museum. Also, if you're expecting to see objects from ancient Akrotiri, you won't find them in the ruins, they've been removed to the museum. One of the highlight pieces that can be found here is a large fresco depicting two Minoan maidens picking wild Saffron - the image is famous in the culture of Santorini.

Admission to the museum is €3. It's open to the public from the 1st of May to the 31st of October, and Monday through Saturday from 10:00 am to 4:00 pm. The museum is closed on Sundays. For a thorough exploration of the museum give yourself 45 minutes or more.

🌍 Akrotiri Ruins

84700, Greece

High in the island's cliffs, through vineyards and volcanic ash alike, likes the "ancient Pompeii of Santorini," the ruins at Akrotiri. The ancient Minoan stronghold of Akrotiri was a peaceful, prosperous city on the Aegean before its daily activity was suddenly interrupted by the Minoan Explosion of 1648 B.C. Up until this point, the island was perfectly round, but with the volcanic eruption came the formation of the sunken caldera, with much of Santorini becoming lost to the sea.

SANTORINI TRAVEL GUIDE

And for a very long time, it was believed that Akrotiri had been lost as well. But in 1860, it was rediscovered while the island was being mined for volcanic ash in the building of the Suez Canal. Due to safety restrictions, the site was closed for the last few years; but after extensive work it was brought back up to speed, and in 2012 was reopened to the public.

The site offers a rare look into the ancient Theran lifestyle, and although most of the artifacts have been removed to Athens or the Museum of Historic Thera at Santorini, the outlay is still there. Visitors have the opportunity to walk don Akrotiri's main stree, alongside historic warehouses and earthenware vessels.

SANTORINI TRAVEL GUIDE

There are tour buses and regular buses that make the steep ascent from the bottom of the cliffs. It is open from Tuesday to Sunday (closed Mondays) from 10:00 am to 5:00 pm. The walkthrough takes about 1 hour, and entrance to the grounds is €8.

🌏 Thirasia

Thirasia was once a part of the Santorini mainland before the Thera Eruption formed the sunken caldera. For the next two millennia, Thirasia has remained predominately untouched by the lifestyle of the Santorini mainland, which has been much to its benefit. Thirasia possesses a permanent population of 150 people, and its economy is dependent upon the fishing trade primarily. The island is very small, only 9 square miles, with 4 main settlements.

SANTORINI TRAVEL GUIDE

Boats to the island leave from Oia daily, and are more frequent in summer. In Oia visitors can wander the charming streets of Thirasia, look at the colorful houses and gardens, in addition to quaint churches. Also, guests can grab a bite to eat at one of the welcoming tavernas, or take a dip in the hot springs.

🌐 Open Air Cinema, Kimari

Main Road, Kamari

84700, Greece

+30 22860 31974

http://www.cinekamari.gr/

Ever since the ancient world of Sophocles, Aeschylus, and Euripides Grecian theater has always been best staged outdoors. With the Open Air Cinema in Kimari, this

SANTORINI TRAVEL GUIDE

legacy continues. For a decade now, the Open Air Cinema has been a hot spot in Kamari.

All through the summer, the cinema plays popular international movies in a unique venue. Guests can grab a drink or a snack from the onsite bar, cosy up in one of the seats, and watch movies beneath the stars.

Show schedules vary, but usually they begin at 9:30 pm, and there's a bus stop near the venue. Tickets to the showings are €7, and movies that have been shown in the past include Star Trek and Mamma Mia. It's fun, and different, a great way to spend the odd evening while in Santorini.

SANTORINI TRAVEL GUIDE

🌐 Ancient Thera

There is not just one but two remarkable ancient historic sites on the island of Santorini. The first is at Akrotiri, and the other at Thera. Situated on top of the Messa Vouno Mountains, ancient Thera was a Hellenistic enclave operated by the Spartans. It existed on this site until the mid-Byzantine era, and was chosen for its incredible height. This height was essential for surveying the surrounding sea, to have enough warning against potential invaders.

Structures on the site include the remains of ancient temples, an amphitheater, and the church of Saint Stephens. Taking a tour is recommended, as you will receive a more thorough education on the lives of those from 800 B.C. Buses leave from Kamari every day except for Monday, starting at 8:30 and ending at 12:30. The grounds close each day at 2:30. Tours are priced at €10 per person.

🌐 Santorini Volcano

Many times per day tour buses depart from Firá to go to the Santorini volcano at Palea Kameni. It is a 2000 years old active volcano. A newer, 500 year old volcano exists on the uninhabited island of Nea Kameni, but the older of the two is certainly the more popular. Visitors can wander along the black lava sides of the ancient wonder, explore the crater, and witness openings in the earth caused by the steam of the underground sulphur. One of the "hot spots" of the Palea Kameni are the volcano's natural hot springs, renowned for their healing properties and beneficial effects on skin.

SANTORINI TRAVEL GUIDE

From the apex of the volcano, you can see stunning views of the surrounding islands, with the picturesque sights of Oia and Firá nestled into the magnificent cliffside. Tickets to the volcano can be purchased right in Firá harbor, at the docks, for about €15 per person.

🌎 Thira Maritime Museum

Oia, Santorini, Greece, 84702

+30 22860 71156

In the traditional town of Oia in Santorini you will find another interesting museum, showcasing the cultural history of this magnificent place. It traces the Hellenistic Merchant Marine and Maritime History of the island, beginning in the 18th century up to the present day.

SANTORINI TRAVEL GUIDE

It is housed in a luxurious mansion that has been restored and converted for the purposes of the museum. Once inside, visitors can view models of old Theran ships, figureheads, ancient maps, cannons, and rare photographs amongst other artifacts of the featured time period.

A trip to the Thira Maritime Museum in Oia is a fascinating excursion into the history of Santorini's seafaring days, and although it wouldn't be the first thing you did while visiting Santorini, it's a great way to spend an afternoon if by chance the weather is not ideal. Admission to the site is €3, and it is open Wednesday through Monday from 10:00 am to 2:00 pm, and again from 5:00 pm to 8:00 pm.

SANTORINI TRAVEL GUIDE

🌍 Monastery of Profitis Ilias, Pyrgos

Pyrgos, 847 00, Greece

+30 22860 31812

The highest point of Santorini can be found in the village of Pyrgos, atop Mount Profitis Illus. Situated at this apex is a Monastery named for the mountain on which it's located. The Monastery of Profitis Ilias has existed on this site since 1711, and in its zenith was dedicated to the prophet Elijah. It thrived for more than one hundred years, before it began facing troubles in the late 19th century. Then, just when it had recovered, it was further wrecked by the volcano of 1956.

However, the monastery was seen as a significant cultural site for the island of Santorini, and it has underwent

SANTORINI TRAVEL GUIDE

extensive renovations over the last few years. One of the most noteworthy parts of the structure is the bell tower, a striking example of the island's unique architecture. It is now open as a museum, a collection of icons and relics, for the public to peruse. The museum itself is open from April to October, from 10:00 am to 4:00 pm.

Many people visit the Monastery not for the collections, however, but for the panoramic views of the horizon. From the summit it is possible to see as far away as Crete, an incredible 100km distant, in addition to the whole of Santorini.

SANTORINI TRAVEL GUIDE

SANTORINI TRAVEL GUIDE

Budget Tips

Accommodation

Finding a place to stay in Santorini can be extremely difficult, especially at certain times of the year. To stay ahead of the crowds, shop around for the best prices, and book early. Hotels in the region offer a wealth of options, everything from picturesque seaside villas to condos overlooking volcanos. No matter what your taste or style, whether you want a bungalow in Kamari or a white walled luxury hotel in Oia, there's a place for you in Santorini.

Zorzis Hotel, Perissa

Perissa 84700, Greece

+011 30 2286 081104

http://www.santorinizorzis.com/

€60-€110

SANTORINI TRAVEL GUIDE

Perissa is known for its stunning black pebble beach, and the Zorzis Hotel for its location in reference to this unique natural wonder.

It has received multiple awards for its cleanliness, and its Grecian decor adds a lively touch to each room. Considering its location, quality, and staff friendliness, you can't beat the price. It's one of the most affordable hotels on Santorini, and it's one of the best.

Mediterranean Beach Hotel, Kamari

Agia Paraskevi, Kamari, Santorini 84700

http://www.mediterraneanbeach.eu/

€100-€150

SANTORINI TRAVEL GUIDE

The Mediterranean Beach Hotel offers beautiful accommodations at reasonable prices. The staff is often available and willing to help, many of them fluent in multiple languages, and the rooms are extremely clean and well cared for. Also, the hotel is located close to the beach, and has extensive restaurant facilities. Many room packages come inclusive with free drinks and meals on premises as well.

Katikies, Oia

Oia 84702, Greece

+22860/71-401

www.katikies.com

€180-€250

Katikies in Oia is the ideal romantic getaway, perfect for

SANTORINI TRAVEL GUIDE

couples looking for seclusion, escape, and spectacular views of the Aegean Sea.

The architecture resembles the stunning outlay of the surrounding city, with elegant white walls and brilliant decor. The hotel has been been built directly into the cliffs of the caldera, which means no separation between you and world-famous views. Luxurious settings combined with a 5 star service make Katikies a stellar choice for your stay in Santorini.

Caldera's Lillum Villa, Fira

Fira, Fira 84700, Greece

+011 30 2286 025333

http://www.lilium-v.gr/

€145-€170

SANTORINI TRAVEL GUIDE

The beautiful, pervasive landscape of Santorini allows for many charming accommodations to coexist within the same small space. Another jewel of the island, found in Fira, is the idyllic Lillum Villa. Like its name suggests, the villa is built into the caldera cliffs, providing the essential views that every stay in Santorini deserves. Amenities include free breakfast, large swimming pool, spacious rooms, and a jacuzzi.

160° Thea Hotel, Oia

Oía, 84700 Santorini, Greece

+30 22860 71832

http://www.160thea.gr/en/

€180-€220

Located in the gorgeous town of Oia, 160° Thea is a panoramic tribute to the glory of the Aegean Sea. It's

SANTORINI TRAVEL GUIDE

clean, comfortable, and offers a series of fantastic perks. First, you are served breakfast each morning in your suite; second, upon offering you are provided with a complimentary welcome drink; and thirdly, there's free Wi-Fi, a rarity on the island. Plus, many of the suites come with balconies, giving guests their own secluded view of the volcano, faraway cliffs, and sea.

🌍 Restaurants, Cafés & Bars

Greek food is lamb, seafood, beef tossed in spices, braised in yogurt, and served with the freshest, most delicious of ingredients. Santorini has adopted influences from many parts of the Mediterranean, and many restaurants sport an eclectic menu with unique takes on old favorites. But the thing that Santorini does best, other than its wonderful tomatoes, and this is almost entirely due to its location in the sea, is certainly seafood. Freshly caught fish in the morning are sold to restauranteurs that same day, or in some cases, the fishermen own the taverna where the fish is to be sold. It's a fun, friendly atmosphere provided in Santorini, one that's Greek at its core.

Palla Kameni Cocktail Bar, Fira

On the Caldera opposite the big church

Next to Arhipelagos Restaurant, Fira, Greece

+22860 22430

http://www.paliakameni.gr/

€3-€15

It's early evening and you're in the mood for a drink, where do you go? For stunning views of the Santorini sunset and some tasty snacks and beverages, Palla Kameni Cocktail Bar offers up a relaxing atmosphere, friendly service, great products, and exceptional location. Whether you're looking for a bite to eat, or just to place to cool your heals and survey the incredible scenery, Palla Kameni is a excellent place to be.

1800 Restaurant, Oia

Odos Nikolaos Nomikos, Oia

+22860-71485

http://www.oia-1800.com/

€15-€30

One of the best restaurants on Santorini, and one of the best places to go for a formal dinner, 1800 restaurant is a foodie haven both enjoyable and affordable. Housed in a gem of Santorini architecture, a neo-classical styled Captain's mansion, 1800 has all the charm of the old world in a modern setting.

SANTORINI TRAVEL GUIDE

Guests can dine in the hall or on the rooftop terrace, both equally charming. A dinner at 1800 is as much a cultural experience as it is a culinary one, and a time that shouldn't be missed while in Santorini.

Roka, Oia

+22860/71-896

http://www.roka.gr/

20-€25

A small family-owned business, Roka is a jewel of Oia serving up local fare hearkening back to simpler times. Fried Sardines, Tomato Croguettes, and decadent Melazane are just a few of the marvelous offerings. It's also not located on the main drag, which means that the experience will be more authentic and less crowded. A meal at Roka means traditional food, fresh ingredients, and friendly service.

Dimitris, Ammoudi

+00 30 22860 71606

€20-€30

There are dozens of seafood restaurants along Ammoudi Bay near Oia, but Dimitris has been reviewed as one of the best. It is a taverna in the Grecian sense, with an extensive menu and generous portion sizes.

The seafood is caught daily, and the amiable staff allow guests to come into the kitchen and choose their fish and the way they want it to be prepared. It's a genuine Greek experience at affordable prices, and at its location across from the water, the atmosphere of the place can't be beat.

SANTORINI TRAVEL GUIDE

Archipelagos, Fira

84700

+30 22860 24509

http://www.archipelagos-santorini.com/

€25-€50

If you're looking for a romantic dinner date destination on your stay in Santorini, then Archipelagos in Fira is a perfect spot for you. Situated on the cliffside overlooking the shining Aegean, Archipelagos offers authentic Greek fare, delicious local wine, and exemplary service. The place tends to be very busy, so make sure that you call ahead for a reservation; and if you manage to get a table, ask for a place in one of the lower rooms close to the windows, allowing you breathtaking views of the Fira horizon.

SANTORINI TRAVEL GUIDE

🌐 Shopping

Shopping in Santorini can be tricky as many of the salesman in the local shops will jump at the opportunity to make a sale, ensuring you that his or her product is the absolute best on the island, whether or not this is actually true is an entirely different story. But in spite of this difficulty, there are two things that Santorini actually does very well, and these are ceramics and wine. There are also large quantities of jewelers in the city center, many of them are expensive, but there is an uncanny variety which continues to have enduring appeal. So, when in the market for something memorable from Santorini, if you shop around, you're sure to find something exceptional.

Kostas Antoniou, Fira

In Spiliotica shopping area, near Archaeological Museum, Fira, Santorini, 84700

SANTORINI TRAVEL GUIDE

+22860/22633

With the the glory of ancient Thera as his muse, Kostas Antoniou has taken an incredible concept and run with it in his jewelry store in Fira. With such an exquisite variety of jewelry in the area, it can often be hard to choose which stores to enter; but with Kostas Antoniou it's a no brainer. Kostas sports the beautiful Triton jewelry line of Gerry Kafieris, that's equally charming and exciting. So, if you're looking for quality aesthetics that's not run of the mill, go to Kostas Antoniou, you won't regret it.

Iama, Oia

Santorini Oia 84702

+3022860 71786

http://www.iamatrade.com/

SANTORINI TRAVEL GUIDE

One of Santorini's premiere industries is their wine, and one of the best wine sellers on the island is at Iama in the town of Oia. They specialize in local wines, especially those produced from Assyrtiko, a white wine grape indigenous to Santorini. They have been on the site for more than 20 years, and have garnered a reputation as being one of the best wine stores on the island. And, the staff is friendly, and more than willing to assist you in any question you might have. They are dedicated to quality, and what you'll find at Iama is nothing less than the best.

Galateas Pottery Studio, Megalochori

Galatea Papageorgiou

E180, Emporeio

Santorini, Greece 84703

+30 22860 82461

SANTORINI TRAVEL GUIDE

http://galateaspottery.wordpress.com/

With Santorini being such a breathtaking place, it is no great wonder that hundreds of unique and talented artists have settled here to make it their permanent home and inspiration. Galatea was born in Greece, grew up in Canada, and then returned to her homeland to study ceramics with the professionals.

And now, she is the owner of the brilliant handmade craft shop in Megalochori. She crafts everything from espresso sets to tiles and vases; and don't worry about trying to lug a delicate piece of handmade pottery around in your luggage, she ships worldwide.

SANTORINI TRAVEL GUIDE

Atlantis Bookstore, Oia

Oia Santorini

T.K. 84702

Kyklades Greece

+30 22860 72346

http://www.atlantisbooks.org/bookshop/

Certainly one of the more peculiar choices on the island, and one of the more original, Atlantis Bookstore in Oia offers an escape to the intellectual looking to catch up on some reading while lounging in the Aegean Sun. Opened in the Spring of 2004 by four English University Students, the bookstore has been an immense success at is is the only bookstore on the island. Conveniently located in the heart of Oia, across from stunning water views, you can stop in, grab a book, and be right back out to catch more rays of sun in no time.

Beach Promenade, Kamari

For souvenir shopping, handcrafts, and eclectic merchandise, head down to the beach walk along Kamari. It's a picturesque setting opposite the glimmering blue coast of the Aegean Sea, and home to many charming shops and boutiques with an assortment of items. Whether you're looking for a trinket, a memento, or something a little more meaningful, a stop in Kamari is the place for you. It's a great way to cool off after spending all day in the radiant sunshine.

SANTORINI TRAVEL GUIDE

Know Before You Go

Entry Requirements

By virtue of the Schengen agreement, travellers from other countries in the European Union do not need a visa when visiting Italy. Additionally Swiss travellers are also exempt. Visitors from certain other countries such as the USA, Canada, Japan, Israel, Australia and New Zealand do not need visas if their stay in Italy does not exceed 90 days. When entering Italy you will be required to make a declaration of presence, either at the airport, or at a police station within eight days of arrival. This applies to visitors from other Schengen countries, as well as those visiting from non-Schengen countries.

Health Insurance

Citizens of other EU countries are covered for emergency health care in Italy. UK residents, as well as visitors from Switzerland are covered by the European Health Insurance Card (EHIC), which can be applied for free of charge. Visitors from non-Schengen countries will need to show proof of private health insurance that is valid for the duration of their stay in

Italy (that offers at least €37,500 coverage), as part of their visa application. No special vaccinations are required.

🌐 Travelling with Pets

Italy participates in the Pet Travel Scheme (PETS) which allows UK residents to travel with their pets without requiring quarantine upon re-entry. Certain conditions will need to be met. The animal will have to be microchipped and up to date on rabies vaccinations. In the case of dogs, a vaccination against canine distemper is also required by the Italian authorities. When travelling from the USA, your pet will need to be microchipped or marked with an identifying tattoo and up to date on rabies vaccinations. An EU Annex IV Veterinary Certificate for Italy will need to be issued by an accredited veterinarian. On arrival in Italy, you can apply for an EU pet passport to ease your travel in other EU countries.

🌐 Airports

Fiumicino – Leonardo da Vinci International Airport (FCO) is one of the busiest airports in Europe and the main international airport of Italy. It is located about 35km southwest of the historical quarter of Rome. Terminal 5 is used for trans-Atlantic and international flights, while Terminals 1, 2 and 3 serve mainly for domestic flights and medium haul flights to other European destinations. Before Leonardo da Vinci replaced it, the **Ciampino–G. B. Pastine International Airport** (CIA) was the main international airport servicing Rome and Italy. It is one of the oldest airports in the country still in use. Although it declined in importance, budget airlines such as Ryanair boosted its air traffic in recent years. The airport is used by Wizz Air, V Bird, Helvetic, Transavia Airlines, Sterling, Ryanair, Thomsonfly, EasyJet, Air Berlin, Hapag-Lloyd Express and Carpatair.

Milan Malpensa Airport (MXP) is the largest of the three airports serving the city of Milan. Located about 40km northwest of Milan's city center, it connects travellers to the regions of Lombardy, Piedmont and Liguria. **Milan Linate Airport** (LIN) is Milan's second international airport. **Venice Marco Polo Airport** (VCE) provides access to the charms of Venice. **Olbia Costa Smeralda Airport** (OLB) is located near Olbia, Sardinia. Main regional airports are **Guglielmo Marconi Airport** (BLQ), an international airport servicing the region of Bologna, **Capodichino Airport** at Naples (NAP), **Pisa International Airport** (PSA), formerly Galileo Galilei Airport, the main airport serving Tuscany, **Sandro Pertini Airport** near Turin (TRN), **Cristoforo Colombo** in Genoa (GOA), **Punta Raisi Airport** in Palermo (PMO), **Vincenzo Bellini Airport** in Catania (CTA) and **Palese Airport** in Bari (BRI).

SANTORINI TRAVEL GUIDE

 Airlines

Alitalia is the flag carrier and national airline of Italy. It has a subsidiary, Alitalia CityLiner, which operates short-haul regional flights. Air Dolomiti is a regional Italian based subsidiary of of the Lufthansa Group. Meridiana is a privately owned airline based at Olbia in Sardinia.

Fiumicino - Leonardo da Vinci International Airport serves as the main hub for Alitalia, which has secondary hubs at Milan Linate and Milan Malpensa Airport. Alitalia CityLiner uses Fiumicino – Leonardo da Vinci International Airport as main hub and has secondary hubs at Milan-Linate, Naples and Trieste. Fiumicino – Leonardo da Vinci International Airport is also one of two primary hubs used by the budget Spanish airline Vueling. Milan Malpensa Airport is one of the largest bases for the British budget airline EasyJet. Venice Airport serves as an Italian base for the Spanish budget airline, Volotea, which provides connections mainly to other destinations in Europe. Olbia Costa Smeralda Airport (OLB), located near Olbia, Sardinia is the primary base of Meridiana, a private Italian Airline in partnership with Air Italia and Fly Egypt.

Currency

Italy's currency is the Euro. It is issued in notes in denominations of €500, €200, €100, €50, €20, €10 and €5.

SANTORINI TRAVEL GUIDE

Coins are issued in denominations of €2, €1, 50c, 20c, 10c, 5c, 2c and 1c.

🌐 Banking & ATMs

Using ATMs or Bancomats, as they are known in Italy, to withdraw money is simple if your ATM card is compatible with the MasterCard/Cirrus or Visa/Plus networks. There is a €250 limit on daily withdrawals. Italian machines are configured for 4-digit PIN numbers, although some machines will be able to handle longer PIN numbers. Bear in mind some Bancomats can run out of cash over weekends and that the more remote villages may not have adequate banking facilities so plan ahead.

🌐 Credit Cards

Credit cards are valid tender in most Italian businesses. While Visa and MasterCard are accepted universally, most tourist oriented businesses also accept American Express and Diners Club. Credit cards issued in Europe are smart cards that that are fitted with a microchip and require a PIN for each transaction. This means that a few ticket machines, self-service vendors and other businesses may not be configured to accept the older magnetic strip credit cards. Do remember to advise your bank or credit card company of your travel plans before leaving.

SANTORINI TRAVEL GUIDE

🌎 Tourist Taxes

Tourist tax varies from city to city, as each municipality sets its own rate. The money is collected by your accommodation and depends on the standard of accommodation. A five star establishment will levy a higher amount than a four star or three star establishment. You can expect to pay somewhere between €1 and €7 per night, with popular destinations like Rome, Venice, Milan and Florence charging a higher overall rate. In some regions, the rate is also adjusted seasonally. Children are usually exempt until at least the age of 10 and sometimes up to the age of 18. In certain areas, disabled persons and their companions also qualify for discounted rates. Tourist tax is payable directly to the hotel or guesthouse before the end of your stay.

🌎 Reclaiming VAT

If you are not from the European Union, you can claim back VAT (Value Added Tax) paid on your purchases in Italy. The VAT rate in Italy is 21 percent and this can be claimed back on your purchases if certain conditions are met. The merchant needs to be partnered with a VAT refund program. This will be indicated if the shop displays a "Tax Free" sign. The shop assistant will fill out a form for reclaiming VAT. When you submit this at the airport, you will receive your refund.

SANTORINI TRAVEL GUIDE

🌎 Tipping Policy

If your bill includes the phrase "coperto e servizio", that means that a service charge or tip is already included. Most waiting staff in Italy are salaried workers, but if the service is excellent, a few euros extra would be appreciated.

🌎 Mobile Phones

Most EU countries, including Italy use the GSM mobile service. This means that most UK phones and some US and Canadian phones and mobile devices will work in Italy. While you could check with your service provider about coverage before you leave, using your own service in roaming mode will involve additional costs. The alternative is to purchase an Italian SIM card to use during your stay in Italy.

Italy has four mobile networks. They are TIM, Wind, Vodafone and Tre (3) and they all provide pre-paid services. TIM offers two tourist options, both priced at €20 (+ €10 for the SIM card) with a choice of two packages - 2Gb data, plus 200 minutes call time or internet access only with a data allowance of 5Gb. Vodafone, Italy's second largest network offers a Vodafone Holiday package including SIM card for €30. They also offer the cheapest roaming rates. Wind offers an Italian Tourist pass for €20 which includes 100 minutes call time and 2Gb data and can be extended with a restart option for an extra €10.

To purchase a local SIM card, you will need to show your passport or some other form of identification and provide your residential details in Italy. By law, SIM registration is required prior to activation. Most Italian SIM cards expire after a 90 day period of inactivity. When dialling internationally, remember to use the (+) sign and the code of the country you are connecting to.

Dialling Code

The international dialling code for Italy is +39.

Emergency Numbers

Police: 113
Fire: 115
Ambulance: 118
MasterCard: 800 789 525
Visa: 800 819 014

Public Holidays

1 January: New Year's Day (Capodanno)
6 January: Day of the Epiphany (Epifania)
March-April: Easter Monday (Lunedì dell'Angelo or Pasquetta)
25 April: Liberation Day (Festa della Liberazione)

SANTORINI TRAVEL GUIDE

1 May: International Worker's Day (Festa del Lavoro / Festa dei Lavoratori)

2 June: Republic Day (Festa della Repubblica)

15 August: Assumption Day (Ferragosto / Assunta)

1 November: All Saints Day (Tutti i santi / Ognissanti)

8 December: Immaculate Conception (Immacolata Concezione / Immacolata)

25 December: Christmas Day (Natale)

26 December: St Stephen's Day (Santo Stefano)

A number of Saints days are observed regionally throughout the year.

🌐 Time Zone

Italy falls in the Central European Time Zone. This can be calculated as Greenwich Mean Time/Coordinated Universal Time (GMT/UTC) +2; Eastern Standard Time (North America) -6; Pacific Standard Time (North America) -9.

🌐 Daylight Savings Time

Clocks are set forward one hour on 29 March and set back one hour on 25 October for Daylight Savings Time.

SANTORINI TRAVEL GUIDE

🌍 School Holidays

The academic year begins in mid September and ends in mid June. The summer holiday is from mid June to mid September, although the exact times may vary according to region. There are short breaks around Christmas and New Year and also during Easter. Some regions such as Venice and Trentino have an additional break during February for the carnival season.

🌍 Trading Hours

Trading hours for the majority of shops are from 9am to 12.30pm and then again from 3.30pm to 7.30pm, although in some areas, the second shift may be from 4pm to 8pm instead. The period between 1pm and 4pm is known in Italy as the *riposo*. Large department shops and malls tend to be open from 9am to 9pm, from Monday to Saturday. Post offices are open from 8.30am to 1.30pm from Monday to Saturday. Most shops and many restaurants are closed on Sundays. Banking hours are from 8.30am to 1.30pm and then again from 3pm to 4pm, Monday to Friday. Most restaurants are open from noon till 2.30pm and then again from 7pm till 11pm or midnight, depending on the establishment. Nightclubs open around 10pm, but only liven up after midnight. Closing times vary, but will generally be between 2am and 4am. Museum hours vary, although major sights tend to be open continuously and often up to 7.30pm. Many museums are closed on Mondays.

🌍 Driving Laws

The Italians drive on the right hand side of the road. A driver's licence from any of the European Union member countries is valid in Italy. Visitors from non-EU countries will require an International Driving Permit that must remain current throughout the duration of their stay in Italy.

The speed limit on Italy's autostrade is 130km per hour and 110km per hour on main extra-urban roads, but this is reduced by 20km to 110km and 90km respectively in rainy weather. On secondary extra-urban roads, the speed limit is 90km per hour; on urban highways, it is 70km per hour and on urban roads, the speed limit is 50km per hour. You are not allowed to drive in the ZTL or Limited Traffic Zone (or *zona traffico limitato* in Italian) unless you have a special permit.

Visitors to Italy are allowed to drive their own non-Italian vehicles in the country for a period of up to six months. After this, they will be required to obtain Italian registration with Italian licence plates. Italy has very strict laws against driving under the influence of alcohol. The blood alcohol limit is 0.05 and drivers caught above the limit face penalties such as fines of up to €6000, confiscation of their vehicles, suspension of their licenses and imprisonment of up to 6 months. Breathalyzer tests are routine at accident scenes.

🌐 Drinking Laws

The legal drinking age in Italy is 16. While drinking in public spaces is allowed, public drunkenness is not tolerated. Alcohol is sold in bars, wine shops, liquor stores and grocery shops.

🌐 Smoking Laws

In 2005, Italy implemented a policy banning smoking from public places such as bars, restaurants, nightclubs and working places, limiting it to specially designated smoking rooms. Further legislation banning smoking from parks, beaches and stadiums is being explored.

🌐 Electricity

Electricity: 220 volts

Frequency: 50 Hz

Italian electricity sockets are compatible with the Type L plugs, a plug that features three round pins or prongs, arranged in a straight line. An alternate is the two-pronged Type C Euro adaptor. If travelling from the USA, you will need a power converter or transformer to convert the voltage from 220 to 110, to avoid damage to your appliances. The latest models of many laptops, camcorders, mobile phones and digital cameras are dual-voltage with a built in converter.

🌐 Tourist Information (TI)

There are tourist information (TI) desks at each of the terminals of the Leonardo da Vinci International Airport, as well as interactive Information kiosks with the latest touch-screen technology. In Rome, the tourist office can be found at 5 Via Parigi, near the Termini Station and it is identified as APT, which stands for Azienda provinciale del Turismo. Free maps and brochures of current events are available from tourist kiosks.

Several of the more tourist-oriented regions of Italy offer tourist cards that include admission to most of the city's attractions. While these cards are not free, some offer great value for money. A variety of tourism apps are also available online.

🌐 Food & Drink

Pasta is a central element of many typically Italian dishes, but there are regional varieties and different types of pasta are matched to different sauces. Well known pasta dishes such as lasagne and bolognaise originated in Bologna. Stuffed pasta is popular in the northern part of Italy, while the abundance of

SANTORINI TRAVEL GUIDE

seafood and olives influences southern Italian cuisine. As far as pizza goes, the Italians differentiate between the thicker Neapolitan pizza and the thin crust Roman pizza, as well as white pizza, also known as focaccia and tomato based pizza. Other standards include minestrone soup, risotto, polenta and a variety of cheeses, hams, sausages and salamis. If you are on a budget, consider snacking on stuzzichini with a few drinks during happy hour which is often between 7 and 9pm. The fare can include salami, cheeses, cured meat, mini pizzas, bread, vegetables, pastries or pate. In Italy, Parmesan refers only to cheese originating from the area surrounding Parma. Favorites desserts include tiramisu or Italian gelato.

Italians enjoy relaxing to aperitifs before they settle down to a meal and their favorites are Campari, Aperol or Negroni, the famous Italian cocktail. Wine is enjoyed with dinner. Italy is particularly famous for its red wines. The best known wine regions are Piedmont, which produces robust and dry reds, Tuscany and Alto Adige, where Alpine soil adds a distinctive acidity. After the meal, they settle down to a glass of limoncello, the country's most popular liqueur, or grappa, which is distilled from grape seeds and stems, as digestive. Other options in this class include a nut liqueur, nocino, strawberry based Fragolino Veneto or herbal digestives like gineprino, laurino or mirto. Italians are also fond of coffee. Espresso is drunk through throughout the day, but cappuccino is considered a morning drink. The most popular beers in Italy are Peroni and Moretti.

 Websites

http://vistoperitalia.esteri.it/home/en

This is the website of the Consulate General of Italy. Here you can look up whether you will need a visa and also process your application online.

http://www.italia.it/en/home.html

The official website of Italian tourism

http://www.italia.it/en/useful-info/mobile-apps.html

Select the region of your choice to download a useful mobile app to your phone.

http://www.italylogue.com/tourism

http://italiantourism.com/index.html

http://www.reidsitaly.com/

http://wikitravel.org/en/Italy

https://www.summerinitaly.com/

http://www.accessibleitalianholiday.com/

Planning Italian vacations around the needs of disabled tourists.

Printed in Great Britain
by Amazon